A BIGAMIST
In The Bunch

A BIGAMIST
In The Bunch

Orville Wilbur and Nettie Drake:
*How their 19th century secret affected
one of New England's oldest families*

Jean Stone

Genealogy House
Amherst, Massachusetts

A Bigamist in the Bunch

Copyright 2014 by Jean Stone

Cover and Book Design
Douglas Lufkin
Lufkin Graphic Designs
www.LufkinGraphics.com

No portion of this book may be reproduced or used in any form, or by any means, without prior written permission of the publisher.

Genealogy House
A division of White River Press
P.O. Box 3561
Amherst, MA 01004

www.genealogyhouse.net

ISBN: 978-1-887043-13-7

Azel Drake and cover photo from the author's collection.

A BIGAMIST
In The Bunch

Azel Whitcomb Drake
1894-1970

Introduction

My grandfather, Azel Drake, was the coolest grandpa on the planet. He was a big man—well over six feet tall—with a wide girth and huge feet and a great smile that easily slipped into a hearty laugh. He had blue eyes that really, truly, twinkled, and a mass of hair that remained white and full even when he died a few weeks before he turned 76.

When I was a kid, I loved riding with him to pick up eggs from a farm in Chester, Massachusetts and to Granville, Massachusetts for a block of cheese that he proclaimed was the "best cheddar anywhere." He pronounced it "cheddah," thanks to his Boston-area roots. The eggs were for Grandma's baking (congo bars, streusel coffee cake, and ginger snap cookies); the cheddar was for grilled cheese sandwiches on Sunday nights and for small wedges to accompany thick slices of Grandma's apple pie.

Grandpa was a "joiner," and he had a lot of friends. He was active in the Congregational church Men's Club and the town Form Club—I have no idea what the Form Club was, I only was remember that he went to meetings.

He was a Mason, too. When one of his friends arrived to pick him up on Lodge Nights, anyone in viewing distance was treated to the sight of Grandpa folding his big body seemingly a million ways then climbing into the man's Volkswagen Beetle.

He loved telling stories, which might or might not be true (one could never be quite sure).

He was a proud man who had worked for the railroad all his adult life; his long, denim overalls and dark charcoal cardigan seemed to hang in perpetuity from a hook on the back of the kitchen door, always sprinkling a little coal dust on the linoleum that Grandma worked so hard to keep clean.

Grandpa always kept a red bandana in the pocket of his overalls. On Saturday afternoons, my father often drove me to the crossing down by the paper mill where we'd wait for the Boston and Albany (the B & A, they called it) to rumble past, where Grandpa would wave that red bandana out the window of the iron engine and blow the whistle just for me.

Before I went off to college, he quietly took me into the front room of the house on Field Street that he'd bought in 1939. Grandma's piano stood in one corner of the room, the same corner where my parents had said their wedding vows as they'd stood between two candelabras that had been borrowed from the church.

When he was certain no one had followed us into the room, Grandpa handed me a twenty-dollar bill. "Put this in your shoe," he said. "If you keep it there, no one can ever say that you are broke."

At the time, it seemed like an odd remark, coming from this big, happy man who had supported a family of four children through the Great Depression and boasted that he'd never spent a day out of work. Today, I might analyze his comment differently; knowing more about the man's background, I have a better frame of reference. Today, I would have realized that my grandfather no doubt worried about money most of his life, and, even more, he worried about what others thought about him.

These years later, as I now know at least in part about the obstacles he overcame, I have a clearer picture of the man. And in that picture, my grandfather has gained even greater respect from me, because he had refused to live a life weighed down by painful family secrets.

What a wonderful example of courage for our generations yet to come.

Thanks, Grandpa Drake.

Jean (Bozenhard) Stone
November 2014

A Bigamist in the Bunch

Orville Wilbur was born in Trescott, Washington County, Maine on 18 March 1862 and died in South Berwick, Maine on 24 November 1943 of intestinal obstruction due to carcinoma of the large bowel. The more we have learned about Orville, my great-grandfather on my mother's side, the more perplexing it is that he lived to be 81 years of age without having been hanged, shot, or at the very least, chased out of New England to parts unknown.

When I was young, details about Orville were locked in the family cedar chest, far from the eyes of Azel's curious grandchildren. Somehow we learned that Orville and my grandfather, Azel, had different last names: Orville's was Wilbur; Azel's was Drake. I might have been twelve or thirteen when my mother explained it to me.

"Grandpa's father was a sea captain," she said one rainy afternoon when I came home from school. We sat at the maple kitchen table with the salmon-colored oilcloth covering. My mother drank tea while I ate a peach. "His mother's name was Nettie. They lived in a small town called Bedford, Massachusetts, northwest of Boston. Orville and Nettie had three children. Your grandfather was the oldest; he had a sister, Ethel, and another one, Ruth. Sometimes, your great-grandfather, Orville, left the family for weeks at a time. They all thought he was working on a boat out of Boston that carried all kinds of New England-made products down the east coast to the southern states."

I started to ask what kinds of products, but my mother put a finger to her lips as if asking me to hold my questions until she was done.

"When your grandfather was about fourteen, his mother learned that Orville was not a sea captain and was not transporting goods to the south. She found out he was hopping a boat that went up the coast to Maine, where he was married to another woman."

I remember that juice from the peach trickled up my arm as I sat there and stared at my mother. "What?" I finally asked.

My mother nodded, stood up, and carried her teacup to the sink. "Grandpa's mother— your great-grandmother— Nettie, took back her maiden name, which was Drake. She changed Grandpa's name from Azel Drake Wilbur to Azel Whitcomb Drake."

I commented that "Whitcomb" was a strange middle name.

"Nettie's mother's first name was Sophronia…her maiden name was Whitcomb."

So when Azel had been born Azel Wilbur, Nettie had given him her maiden name of Drake as a middle name; when she changed his name to Azel Drake, his middle name then became her mother's maiden name. I supposed it made some kind of sense.

"Anyway," my mother continued, "Nettie had an older sister—I think her name was Ella—who owned a corset factory in Boston and was rather wealthy. The sister gave Nettie the money to leave her shame behind in Bedford, and move with her three children to western Massachusetts. They settled in Easthampton, where your grandfather went to Williston Seminary. That's where he met your grandmother. The school was for boys only, but your grandmother's father was the music teacher, so she was allowed to take classes there."

That part wasn't news: I had known that my grandparents had met at Williston. The rest, however, left me stunned.

"So Grandpa's father was a bigamist?" I asked.

My mother nodded again and wiped her hands on her apron. "But you're never to mention this to anyone," she said. "Not Grandma. And certainly not Grandpa. He hates his father and has had nothing to do with him since he moved out here. Besides, Orville must be dead by now."

I never mentioned the family secret to "anyone" except my sister, Joan, and my cousin, Linda. They were older than I was (by two and a half and one and a half years) and had already heard pretty much the same story. Imagine my surprise when, twenty or more years later, long after my grandparents and my mother had died, I sat going through old photographs with my mother's youngest sister, Lois, who smiled and held out a sepia-toned photo. "I'll bet you've never seen this," she said.

The picture showed a small gathering on a summer afternoon. A table had been set up under a large shade tree: a teenage girl wearing a mid-calf, plain cotton dress caught my eye first. She had short, dark hair and a serious look. I recognized her as my mother. A younger version of my mother stood beside her; and then a girl, eight or nine, who had my Aunt Lois's trademark ringlets held in place by a long piece of ribbon. An older woman—my grandmother, I supposed, though it was difficult to see her face under her wide-brimmed straw hat—sat at the table next to a pitcher of something, a few cups, and a wicker hamper. A five or six year old boy who must have been my uncle stood close to her. But the most haunting image in the photo was that of an old man. He had a long, white beard and wore shabby clothes. He sat off to one side, his hands planted on the top of a crude-looking cane that he held close to what looked like his wooden leg.

"That's your great-grandfather Orville," my aunt Lois said. "Have you ever heard about him?"

I admitted I had. "But is this Grandma? And my mother?"

"And Shirley; your uncle, Bob; and me," Aunt Lois said, verifying my mother's siblings.

"But I didn't think Grandpa ever saw his father after…well…after they'd left Bedford."

"He didn't. But somehow Grandma found out he was living on a poor farm in Maine. I remember we took the train to see him. Grandma's sister, Margaret, came with us. She paid someone to take this picture."

"But why did you go?" I asked.

"Your grandma thought it was only right that he meet his grandchildren before he died. We stayed overnight in a guesthouse. I don't know whether or not Grandpa was angry that we went. We never saw or talked about Orville again."

Until recently, that was the full extent of Orville's unpleasant legend. Sadly, I do not know whatever happened to that photograph. But as I began my in-depth genealogy research, I uncovered a few head-scratching "issues" about the story:

1. **TRUE:** Orville Wilbur and Nettie Drake were married in Boston, Massachusetts on 3 December 1892.

2. **TRUE:** They had three children: Azel Drake born 5 May 1894; Ethel Marion born 6 July 1895; Ruth born 22 February 1903.

3. **FALSE:** Orville was not a sea captain, but a farmer.

4. **FALSE:** Nettie did not learn about Orville's "other wife" when Azel was fourteen. Instead, Nettie had found out much earlier when Orville was served divorce papers from one Etta Wilbur at their home in Bedford on 1 October 1893…ten months after Orville and Nettie had married. By then, however, Nettie was two months pregnant with Azel.

5. Etta lived in Lubec, Maine, so at least the part of the legend of him going off to Maine was

probably correct. Thankfully, the couple had no children.

But it wasn't until seven years later, on 29 September 1904, that Nettie booted Orville out of the house and filed for divorce. In the request, she reported Orville was "of vicious temperament and hath been convicted of various assaults and that she is in actual fear of her personal safety." She also feared he might "attempt violence upon her or upon her said minor children." (Of course, we have no way of knowing whether or not that was true, or if poor Nettie was simply trying to avoid ever having to see this guy again.)

And then…someone realized that the paperwork had to be changed into a "nullity of marriage" because they weren't legally married in the first place. I uncovered that document, which is complete with Nettie's signature. I felt very sad when I saw her signature—somehow, this made her seem so much more real, so much more vulnerable. By then she had returned to her maiden name of Drake and had begun to refer to her three children—Azel, Ethel, and Ruth—as also having the Drake surname.

On 4 April 1905 Nettie was granted a "Decree of Nullity" to her marriage in Middlesex Superior Court. The decree stipulated that, when they were married, Nettie believed Orville "had never been married before" but that, even after learning of his first marriage, Nettie and Orville "continued thereafter to live together, neither believing that they were legally married to each other." The decree also cited that "on his repeated promise, and her reliance of that promise" Nettie believed "he would marry her." He did not.

We can only imagine what a difficult time that must have been for Nettie. Yet unlike the family "tale," she did not pack up her family and move to western Massachusetts, but remained in Bedford. From September 1910 to June 1912, my grandfather was a student at New Church School in Waltham, Massachusetts. When he was eighteen, he did, indeed make his way to western Massachusetts to study at Williston Seminary in Easthampton. Nettie's generous corset business-minded sister supposedly paid for his education. (Note: In later research at Williston, I learned that my grandfather only spent one year at the seminary, and was ultimately asked to leave due to "behavioral problems.")

Orville disappeared, then resurfaced in South Berwick, Maine, in 1935, probably around the time that picture of the "picnic" was taken. My sister unearthed a document that said Orville had become a resident of Knights Pond Road "Town Farm"…another term for a "poorhouse." The Town of South Berwick Annual Reports list yearly expenses paid on behalf of Orville E. Wilbur as follows:

    1935 Feb. 1 . . . . $ 234.35

    1936 Feb. 1 . . . . $130.40

    1937 Feb. 1 . . . . $307.36

    1938 Feb. 1 . . . . $160.41

    1939 Feb. 1 . . . . $378.03 *(board)*

    1940 Feb. 1 . . . . $280.90 *(clothing & medicine)*

    1941 Feb. 1 . . . . $40.52 *(board)*

    1942 Feb. 1 . . . . $34.54 *(board)*

1943 Feb. 1 . . . . $20.00 *(board)*

1944 Feb. 1 . . . . $99.79 *(board & medicine)*

1945 Feb. 1 . . . . $15.00

Death—24 Nov 1944

Interestingly, his death certificate reads that he died on 24 Nov 1943, and that he was buried in St. Michael's Cemetery in Rollinsford, New Hampshire on 26 Nov 1943. The discrepancy of dates is odd, but not surprising, as records were occasionally dated incorrectly.

The impact that Orville's life and lies had upon his family continued long past his death. When my grandmother, Mabelle Clark, married my grandfather, Azel Drake, she quite naturally took Drake as her last name. The only problem was, Nettie had never legally changed her last name from Wilbur back to Drake; she had never changed her three children's last names legally, either. In the eyes of the law, "Mabelle Drake" was not a valid name, either. Nor were the names of their four children: Miriam Drake (my mother), Shirley Drake, Lois Drake, or Robert Drake. Apparently, my grandfather never realized this could create a problem at some point in time.

The "point in time" came in January 1949. I cannot find anything to say why the problem arose. By then, however, his daughters Miriam and Shirley had both married, so their last names were legally different (Bozenhard and Franklin, respectively). His daughter, Lois, was 21, but I can't find any record of her name ever being legally changed to Drake. Perhaps my grandfather didn't think that it would matter, as no doubt she would be married one day, anyway. (Within a few years, she did marry and took her husband's last name, Bowen.) However, his son, Robert, was not yet 21, so he became part of the petition to Probate Court in Hampden County Massachusetts that listed the petitioners with the name my grandfather had once wanted to forget:

Azel Drake Wilbur

Mabelle Agnes Wilbur

Robert Whitcomb Wilbur

Interestingly, though her name stayed "Drake," my aunt Lois knew nothing about this legal name change until 1961 when my grandfather applied for his railroad pension. (He had begun as a fireman, then had been promoted to brakeman, then, later, to engineer for the Boston and Albany Railroad.) Lois was widowed and living back home at that time, and saw the paperwork that documented the name change. I don't know if my uncle ever knew that his name had been "changed."

To show that we are a forgiving family, when my sister moved to Maine in the early 1980s, she and her family decided to raise sheep. They had one very sweet, little black sheep. They named him Orville, and they loved him.

The Commonwealth of Massachusetts
OFFICE OF THE SECRETARY OF STATE
WILLIAM FRANCIS GALVIN, SECRETARY
Archives Division   M0028

COPY OF RECORD OF MARRIAGE

I, the undersigned, hereby certify that I am the Secretary of State; that as such I have the custody of the records of marriage required by law to be kept in my office; that among such records is one relating to the marriage of

Orwell E. Wilbur and Nettie M. Drake

and that the following is a true copy of so much of said record as relates to said marriage, namely:

Date of Marriage: December 3, 1892   **Place of Marriage:** Boston

—— GROOM ——   —— BRIDE ——

Name: Orwell E. Wilbur	**Name:** Nettie M. Drake
Age: 29 **Color:** ---	**Age:** 31 **Color:** ---
Residence: Boston	**Residence:** Boston
Number of Marriage: First **Single, Wid, or Divorced:** ---	**Number of Marriage:** First **Single, Wid, or Divorced:** ---
Occupation: Farmer	**Occupation:** at Home
Birthplace: Trescott, Me.	**Birthplace:** Blanchard, Me.
Name of Father: James Wilbur	**Name of Father:** Azel Drake
Mother's Maiden Name: Sarah ---	**Mother's Maiden Name:** Sophronia ---

Name and official station of person by whom married:
Rev. S.H. Winkley Boston

Date of Record: Dec. 5, 1892

And I do hereby certify that the foregoing is a true copy from said records. WITNESS my hand and the GREAT SEAL OF THE COMMONWEALTH at Boston on this 7th day of September 2011

Year: 1892
Vol. 426
Page 294
No. 5279

SECRETARY OF THE COMMONWEALTH

Marriage certificate

The Commonwealth of Massachusetts
COPY OF RECORD OF BIRTH
Town of Bedford

I, the undersigned, hereby certify that I am Clerk of the Town of Bedford; that as such I have custody of the records of births required by law to be kept in my office; that among such records is one relating to the birth of _Azel Drake Wilbur_ and that the following is a true copy of so much of said record as relates to said birth, namely:

Date of Birth _May 2, 1894_
Place of Birth _Bedford, Mass._

Name of Child _Azel Drake Wilbur_
Sex _Male_ Color _White_ If Twin _—_

FATHER
Name _Orville E. Wilbur_
Residence _Bedford, Mass._
Place of Birth _Maine_
Occupation _Farmer_

MOTHER
Maiden Name _Nettie M. Drake_
Residence _Bedford, Mass._
Place of Birth _Maine_

Date of Record _Feb. 1, 1895_

And I do hereby certify that the foregoing is a true copy from said records.

Witness my hand and seal of said Town of Bedford on this _9th_ day of _March_ 19_43_

Arthur E. Carson
Town Clerk

Azel's birth certificate

Commonwealth of Massachusetts.

Middlesex, ss.   Superior Court.

Nettie M. Drake,

otherwise known as Nettie M. Wilbur

vs.

Orivell E. Wilbur.

DECREE OF NULLITY.

    This cause came on to be heard at this sitting, and thereupon, on consideration thereof, the Court find that the marriage contract set out in the petition was entered into by the petitioner, who was capable of contracting this marriage with the full belief that the respondent had never been married before, and that before the impediment to their marriage was removed, she discovered and he knew that his former wife had not then obtained, but was then applying for a divorce. The petitioner and respondent continued thereafter to live together, neither believing that they were legally married to each other, but on his repeated promise, and her reliance on that promise, that after the impediment to his marriage to her should be removed, he would marry her. After the removal of the impediment to their marriage, on his refusal to carry out his promise, she brought this petition.

    The marriage is declared void by reason of the prior marriage of the Respondent.

    The Petitioner is to have the custody of the minor children, Azel Drake, Ethel Marion and Ruth.

                                       By the Court,

April 11-1905   Ralph N. Smith
                                                                          Ass't Clerk.

Nettie's request for divorce

COMMONWEALTH OF MASSACHUSETTS.

MIDDLESEX, ss.   SUPERIOR COURT.
                                                  DIVORCE SESSION.

Nettie M. Wilbur -vs- Orivell E. Wilbur

Now comes the libellant and moves to amend her said libel for divorce by striking out the whole of the same except the caption thereof and substituting therefor the following libel for nullity of marriage.

Respectfully libels and represents Nettie M. Drake otherwise known as Nettie M. Wilbur, of Bedford, in the County of Middlesex that she was married in form of law but not in legal effect to Orivell E. Wilbur of said Bedford, now at Boston in our County of Suffolk, the third day of December in the year of our Lord eighteen hundred and ninety two.

That at the time of said pretended marriage said Orivell E. Wilbur was incapable of contracting marriage with your libellant for that prior to that time, to wit, on the twenty sixth day of June in the year of our Lord eighteen hundred and eighty eight, said Orivell E. Wilbur was married to Etta Wilbur at Lubec, in the State of Maine, and at the time of said pretended marriage to your libellant, said Etta . Wilbur was and is still living.

That there have been born of said pretended marriage three children, Azel Drake, born May 2nd, 1894, Ethel Marion, born July 6th 1895 and Ruth born February 22nd, 1903

That said Etta Wilbur was divorced from said Orivell E. Wilbur on the twelfth day of October, eighteen hundred and ninety three in the State of Maine.

That your libellant entered into said pretended marriage in good faith and in the full belief that said libellee was capable

Request to change from divorce to nullity

of contracting said marriage.

WHEREFORE your libellant prays that said pretended marriage may by the decree of this court be declared null and void and that the care and custody of said minor children may be committed and decreed to your libellant and that the said minor children may be decreed to be the legitimate issue of your libellant.

Nettie M. Drake.

To the Honorable the Justices of the Superior Court within and for the County of Middlesex:

RESPECTFULLY libels and represents Nettie M. Wilbur of Bedford in said County, that she was lawfully married to Orivell E. Wilbur of said Bedford now

at Boston in our County of Suffolk on the third day of December A.D 1892, and thereafterwards your libellant and the said Orivell E. Wilbur lived together as husband and wife in this Commonwealth, to wit, at said Boston and last at said Bedford

that your libellant has always been faithful to her marriage vows and obligations, but the said Orivell E. Wilbur being wholly regardless of the same, at said Bedford at various times personally assaulted your libellant and hath been guilty of cruel and abusive treatment and of extreme cruelty toward your libellant, and your petitioner further represents that there hath been born to her of said marriage three minor children viz:-Azel Drake Wilbur born May 2, 1894, Ethel Marian Wilbur born June 6, 1895, and Ruth Wilbur born Feb.22, 1903, all being now in the custody of your libellant. And your libellant says that the said libellee is of vicious temperament and hath been convicted of various assaults and that she is in actual fear of her personal safety, and that the said libellee may attempt violence upon her or upon her said minor children, wherefore she prays that this Honorable Court will issue its restraining order, restraining the said respondent from interfering with the personal liberty of this libellant pendente lite or from in any way interfering with or disturbing your libellant in this case; In the care custody or control of said minor children.

Wherefore your libellant prays that a divorce from the bonds of matrimony may be decreed between your libellant and the said Orivell E. Wilbur, and that the care and custody of said minor children may be committed and decreed to your libellant.

Dated this twenty-ninth day of September A.D. 1904.

Nettie M. Wilbur

Request for decree of nullity

COMMONWEALTH OF MASSACHUSETTS

HAMPDEN ss

At a Probate Court held at Springfield, in and for the County of Hampden, on the ...eighteenth... day of ...January... in the year one thousand nine hundred forty-nine.

ON the petition of ...Azel Drake Wilbur...
and ...Mabelle Agnes Wilbur..., his wife,
and ...Robert Whitcomb Wilbur, minor,
by ...Azel Drake Wilbur, his... father and next friend,
of ...West Springfield, in said County, praying that their names may be changed as follows:
Azel Drake Wilbur to Azel Whitcomb Drake
Mabelle Agnes Wilbur to Mabelle Agnes Drake
Robert Whitcomb Wilbur to Robert Whitcomb Drake

public notice having been given, according to the order of the Court, and no objection being made:

It is decreed that their names be changed, as prayed for, which names they shall hereafter bear, and which shall be their legal names.

_____ Judge of Probate Court.

Petition for name change

The Ancestors & Descendants of Azel Drake Wilbur
(aka Azel Whitcomb Drake)

GENERATION 1—FATHER'S SIDE

1. **BENJAMIN[1] WILBUR** was born around 1786 in Dorchester, Province of Nova Scotia, Canada and died 25 April 1863. According to Town Records of Dennysville, Maine, he was in Dennysville in 1804 and was taxed on Plantation #2, but was not qualified to vote for Senators and Representatives because he was not a citizen. (Benjamin lived in the part of Dennysville that is now called Pembroke. The Native American name was "Pennamaquon," and it was settled in 1794. It remained part of Dennysville until it incorporated in February 1832.) Benjamin married **ELIZABETH BLACKWOOD**, daughter of James Blackwood and his wife, Nancy in early 1812. The marriage was recorded on 12 March 1812. She was born on 11 July 1790. In September 1822 he applied to the Court to become a naturalized citizen of the United States. He listed his occupation as a farmer. His wife died 2 August 1834; no record can be found of him remarrying. He was 77 when he died.

Benjamin Wilbur and Elizabeth Blackwood had the following children:

1. WILLIAM WILBUR born 7 Sept. 1812. He was a sea captain and rum runner. He died 28 Sept. 1887, supposedly murdered by his second wife when she put ground glass in his food.

2. BENJAMIN WILBUR born 23 Sept. 1814. He was a Baptist preacher.

3. **JAMES[2] BLACKWOOD WILBUR** born 24 Oct. 1816 in Pembroke, Maine. His occupation was a farmer. He married 1st SARAH JANE LEIGHTON on 1 Sept. 1846, 2nd (MARY) ELIZABETH, and 3rd MARIA _____. He died 13 April 1882

4. AARON WILBUR born 20 June 1819

5. JOSIAH EATON WILBUR born 8 June 1822

6. HERMAN NICKERSON WILBUR born 14 July 1823

7. THOMAS GRAY WILBUR born 21 Aug. 1825

8. DAVID WILBUR born 15 Nov. 1827

9. SARAH ELIZABETH WILBUR born 13 June 1830

10. JANE MAHAR WILBUR born 15 March 1833

GENERATION 1—MOTHER'S SIDE

1. **ISAAC^1 DOTEN DRAKE** was born 22 September 1805 in Bridgewater, Massachusetts and died 10 May 1838 in Auburn, Maine. He married SALLY WOODMAN on 8 January 1829 in Mercer, Maine.

   Isaac Doten Drake and Sally Woodman had the following children:

   1. EDWARD RUSSELL DRAKE born in Nov. 1830
   2. **AZAEL^2 WOODMAN DRAKE** born 1 April 1832
   3. BETSY JANE DRAKE born 26 Aug. 1833

GENERATION 2—FATHER'S SIDE

2. **JAMES^2 BLACKWOOD WILBUR** (Benjamin^1) was born 24 October 1816 in Pembroke, Maine and died 13 April 1882. His occupation was a farmer. He married (1) **SARAH JANE LEIGHTON** on 1 September 1846, (2) (MARY) ELIZABETH, and (3) MARIA _____.

   James Blackwood Wilbur and Sarah Jane Leighton had the following children:

   1. MARY E. WILBUR born in 1848; died 5 April 1866
   2. STEPHEN E. WILBUR born in 1850; died before 1860

3. ACEY LAURA WILBUR born in 1853; died 1854

4. ELIJAH WILLIAM WILBUR born in 1855—a cobbler and harness maker

5. ELIZA H. WILBUR born in 1858

6. **ORVILLE³ WILBUR** born 18 March 1862

James Blackwood Wilbur and (Mary) Elizabeth had the following children:

7. WILLLIAM H. WILBUR born 7 April 1872

James Blackwood Wilbur and Maria _____ had the following children:

8. JAMES W. WILBUR born 4 Dec. 1878

GENERATION 2—MOTHER'S SIDE

2. **AZAEL² WOODMAN DRAKE** was born 1 April 1832 in Minot, Maine and died on 25 February 1919 in Abbott, Maine. He married SOPHRONIA L. WHITCOMB of Mercer, Maine on 9 November 1857. His occupation was listed as a "laborer." He enlisted in Co.H, 11th Reg., Infantry, Maine Volunteers on 1 August 1863. His discharge reads: "M.O. & Hon. 26 March 1866." His physical description was given as 5' 6-1/2", sandy complexion, blue eyes, brown hair. At some unknown date, he and Sophronia were divorced.

Azael² Woodman Drake and Sophronia L. Whitcomb had the following children:

1. ELLA AUGUSTA DRAKE
2. CHARLOTTE DRAKE (died young)
3. **NETTIE³ MELISSA DRAKE** born 14 April 1861

GENERATION 3

3. **ORVILLE³ WILBUR** (James² Benjamin¹) was born 18 March 1862 in Trescott, Washington County, Maine, and died 23 November 1943 in South Berwick, Maine.

His occupation is listed as a farmer; because no records show him having owned any land in the state of Maine, it is assumed he was a tenant farmer. Orville's mother, Sarah Jane Leighton died in January 1866 when he was not quite four years old. His father, James Blackwood Wilbur, married by 1870 and in 1876 his stepmother, (Mary) Elizabeth died. His father took his third wife, Maria, in 1877. Five years later, on 13 April 1886, his father died. Orville was 20 years old. And he disappeared. He resurfaced in Lubec, Maine, when he married (1) (Mrs.) Etta Leighton on 26 April 1888. They had no known children. He deserted her 26 March 1890. She filed for divorce 1 October 1893 in Machias, Maine, stating "He is guilty of extreme cruelty…obscene and profane language…violently and repeatedly laid hands upon her…dragged and beat her about." Papers were served to him on Main

Street, Bedford, Massachusetts where he was living and was already married to (2) **NETTIE³ MELISSA DRAKE**, having wed on 3 December 1892. Nettie died 19 October 1914 of breast cancer.

Orville Wilbur and Nettie Melissa Drake had the following children:

1. **AZEL⁴ DRAKE WILBUR** born 2 May 1894

2. ETHEL MARION WILBUR born 6 July 1895

3. RUTH S. WILBUR born 22 Feb. 1903

Nettie had her marriage to Orville annulled in 1905. Soon after, Orville visited his brother, ELIJAH WILLIAM WILBUR in Rangeley, Maine, according to a 1984 interview with Elijah's daughter, Sarah, who remembered her father's anger over Orville's situation. Sarah said her father went into a violent rage and "threw" Orville out of the house.

The next documentation of the whereabouts of ORVILLE WILBUR is when he was a resident of Knights Pond Road Town Farm—the poorhouse—in South Berwick, Maine. He died 24 November 1943 and was buried in St. Michael's Cemetery in Rollinsford, New Hampshire on 26 November 1943. His death certificate notes the cause of death as "intestinal obstruction due to carcinoma of the large bowel."

GENERATION 4

4. **AZEL[4] DRAKE WILBUR**, (Orville[3] James[2] Benjamin[1]) aka **AZEL WHITCOMB DRAKE** was born 2 May 1894 in Bedford, Massachusetts to Orville Wilbur and Nettie Melissa Drake. He died 18 April 1970 of heart disease. He married **MABELLE AGNES CLARK** of Easthampton, Massachusetts on 5 April 1916. He attended New Church School in Waltham, Massachusetts from September 1910 to June 1912, and Williston Seminary in Easthampton, Massachusetts from September 1912 to June 1913. He began his railroad career as a fireman, then worked his way up to brakeman, then to engineer on the Boston and Albany Railroad. When his parents split up in 1905, his mother changed his name to Azel Whitcomb Drake, although this was not accomplished legally until 18 January 1949. Mabelle Agnes Clark died 12 November 1973.

Azel Whitcomb Drake and Mabelle Agnes Clark had the following children:

1. **MIRIAM[5] RUTH DRAKE** born 30 Sept. 1918; died 19 July 1982
2. SHIRLEY AGNES DRAKE born in April 1920; died in June 2002
3. LOIS BEVERLY DRAKE born 19 July 1920; died 5 May 2007
4. ROBERT WHITCOMB DRAKE born 3 April 1928; died 21 Oct 1992

GENERATION 5

5. **MIRIAM⁵ RUTH DRAKE** (Azel⁴ Orville³ James² Benjamin¹) was born 30 September 1918 in Springfield, Massachusetts and died 19 July 1982 in Holyoke, Massachusetts. She was married 31 January 1941 to STEWART GEORGE BOZENHARD in West Springfield, Massachusetts. He was born 12 July 1917 and died 8 September 1974. She had been employed as a clerk at Massachusetts Mutual Life Insurance Co. In 1943, during World War II, the couple relocated to Denver, Colorado where Stewart continued his work for the war effort through his employer, Worthington Pump, Co., of Holyoke, Massachusetts. After the war, they returned to West Springfield, Massachusetts where they lived for the remainder of their lives.

Miriam Ruth Drake and Stewart George Bozenhard had the following children:

1. JOAN ELIZABETH BOZENHARD born 12 July 1945

2. **JEAN⁶ MIRIAM BOZENHARD** born 28 Feb. 1948

GENERATION 6

6. **JEAN[6] MIRIAM BOZENHARD** (Miriam[5] Azel[4] Orville[3] James[2] Benjamin[1]) was born 28 February 1948 in Springfield, Massachusetts to Stewart George Bozenhard and Miriam[5] Ruth Drake. She was married 28 June 1969 to THOMAS ROBERT STONE and divorced 4 July 1973. An advertising copywriter, she owned her own advertising agency from 1978 to 1992 at which time she became a novelist. She had 18 books published beginning in 1992.

> Genealogy prepared by:
> Joan (Bozenhard) Adams
> December 1985

About the Author

Jean Stone is a great-granddaughter of Nettie and Orville. Inspired by the in-depth genealogy research done by her sister, Joan Adams, Jean set out to learn more. The author of 17 novels, one non-fiction book, and countless articles, Jean is also a developmental editor with many additional books to her credit. *The Bigamist in the Bunch*, however, is personal. "It happened in my family," she said. "I wanted to document the truth."

Genealogy House
Publishers of Family History and Genealogy

Genealogy House publishes narrative family histories and genealogies that combine good writing and editing with genealogical research.

By incorporating high editorial and production standards, we maintain the best of traditional publishing and combine it with today's advantages of digital printing and distribution technologies. The result is a process that is professional, efficient, cost effective, flexible, and responsible.

Our goal is to capture the spirit of the people of the past to share with generations to come.

a division of White River Press
Amherst, Massachusetts

www.genealogyhouse.net